CONTEMPORARY LIVING
IN PROVENCE & COTE D'AZUR

DEMEURES CONTEMPORAINES
EN PROVENCE & CÔTE D'AZUR

HEDENDAAGS WONEN
IN PROVENCE & COTE D'AZUR

CONTEMPORARY LIVING
IN PROVENCE & COTE D'AZUR

DEMEURES CONTEMPORAINES
EN PROVENCE ET CÔTE D'AZUR

HEDENDAAGS WONEN
IN PROVENCE & COTE D'AZUR

BETA-PLUS

Printed in China.

FOREWORD

This book will take you on an architectural tour through Provence and the Côte d'Azur, considered by many people to be the most beautiful region of France.
Contemporary architecture and design are the theme of this book: in contrast with the classic Provençal style, we make a case for resolutely modern, streamlined architecture and interiors.

Two tendencies stand out: on the one hand, the renovation and "stripping" of classic *mas*, *bastides* and country houses, which are reduced to their true essence, with the exterior often remaining intact for conservation reasons, and, on the other hand, the construction of uncompromising, visionary villas that make you forget the classic architectural idiom of this region.

Following a visit to a contemporary mas near Dante's "Val d'Enfer" (Les Baux-de-Provence), we stop off at the restored *bastide* of some design enthusiasts near Aix-en-Provence.
The journey then takes us to the Côte d'Azur, with reports from exclusive holiday homes in famous resorts such as Saint-Tropez, Ramatuelle and Cannes.
The book concludes with a trip to an exceptional architect's home in the Massif des Maures.

A different, more contemporary look at "le style provençal".

Wim Pauwels
Publisher

PREFACE

Ce volume est un périple architectural à travers la Provence et la Côte d'Azur, considérée par un grand nombre comme la plus belle région de France.
L'architecture et le design contemporains constituent le fil conducteur de cet ouvrage : contrairement au style provençal classique, ce volume est un plaidoyer en faveur d'une architecture (d'intérieure) épurée, résolument moderne.

Deux tendances se dessinent : d'une part, la rénovation et le "déshabillage" de mas, de bastides et de maisons de campagne classiques pour ne garder que leur essence (l'extérieur est généralement conservé tel quel pour des raisons urbanistiques) et d'autre part, la construction de villas visionnaires, affranchies de compromis, qui font complètement oublier l'idiome architectural classique de cette région.

Après la visite d'un mas contemporain près du Val d'Enfer de Dante (Les Baux-de-Provence), une halte est faite près d'Aix-en-Provence dans la bastide restaurée d'amoureux du design.
Le voyage continue ensuite vers la Côte d'Azur, avec des reportages de résidences de vacances exclusives dans des lieux de villégiature célèbres comme Saint-Tropez, Ramatuelle et Cannes.
L'ouvrage s'achève par une étape dans le Massif des Maures montrant une habitation d'architecte originale.

Un regard différent, contemporain sur "le style provençal".

Wim Pauwels
Éditeur

VOORWOORD

In dit boek wordt een architecturale rondreis gemaakt doorheen de Provence en Côte d'Azur, voor velen aanzien als de mooiste regio van Frankrijk.
Hedendaagse architectuur en design vormen de leidraad in dit boek: in tegenstelling tot de klassieke Provençaalse stijl wordt hier een pleidooi gegeven voor een resoluut moderne, uitgepuurde (interieur)architectuur.

Twee tendenzen tekenen zich daarbij af: enerzijds het renoveren en "uitkleden" van klassieke mas, bastides en landhuizen tot hun ware essentie (waarbij het exterieur om stedebouwkundige redenen vaak intact blijft) en anderzijds het bouwen van compromisloze, visionaire villa's die het klassieke architectuuridioom van deze streek helemaal doen vergeten.

Na het bezoek van een hedendaagse mas nabij Dantes "Val d'Enfer" (Les Baux-de-Provence) wordt halt gehouden in de gerestaureerde bastide van designliefhebbers nabij Aix-en-Provence.
Daarna gaat het richting Azurenkust, met de reportages van exclusieve vakantiehuizen in gerenommeerde vakantie-oorden zoals Saint-Tropez, Ramatuelle en Cannes.
Het boek wordt afgesloten met de uitstap naar een bijzondere architectenwoning in het Massif des Maures.

Een andere, hedendaagsere kijk op "le style provençal".

Wim Pauwels
Uitgever

CONTENTS

SOMMAIRE

INHOUD

CONTEMPORARY LIVING IN A CLASSIC MAS

VIVRE À LA MODE CONTEMPORAINE DANS UN MAS CLASSIQUE

HEDENDAAGS WONEN IN EEN KLASSIEKE MAS

Architect Jean Lemaire (Eygalières) built this mas near Saint-Rémy-de-Provence in 1977 in the typical, classic Provençal style to conform with local planning regulations.
Exactly one quarter of a century after the construction of the house, it was thoroughly renovated and interior designer Aldo Marcone from Grenoble gave the house a refreshing contemporary look.

Ce mas proche de Saint-Rémy-de-Provence a été construit en 1977, en conformité avec les directives urbanistiques locales de l'époque, par l'architecte Jean Lemaire (Eygalières) dans le style provençal classique, typique de la région.
Un quart de siècle exactement après sa construction, le bâtiment a été restauré en profondeur.
L'intérieur a été réaménagé par l'architecte d'intérieur Aldo Marcone, de Grenoble, qui lui a insufflé un surprenant rayonnement contemporain.

Deze mas nabij Saint-Rémy-de-Provence is conform de lokale urbanistieke voorschriften in 1977 gebouwd door architect Jean Lemaire (Eygalières) in de typische, klassieke Provençaalse stijl.
Precies een kwarteeuw na de bouw van de woning werd deze grondig gerenoveerd en kreeg de interieurinrichting van binnenhuisarchitect Aldo Marcone uit Grenoble een verrassend hedendaagse uitstraling.

The *mas* is situated near the Val d'Enfer, the Valley of Hell, a spectacular gorge with rugged rocks and caves by Les Baux de Provence, one of the most beautiful tourist spots in Provence and a source of inspiration for Dante's Inferno in *La Divina Commedia*.

Le mas se situe aux environs immédiats du Val d'Enfer, une gorge spectaculaire, toute en roches et en grottes sauvages, aux alentours des Baux de Provence. La région est un des pôles d'attraction touristique les plus fascinants de la Provence. C'est elle qui a servi de source d'inspiration à l'Enfer de Dante, dans *La Divine Comédie*.

De mas ligt in de nabije omgeving van de Val d'Enfer, een spectaculaire kloof met ruige rotsen en grotten nabij Les Baux de Provence, één van de mooiste toeristische trekpleisters in de Provence en inspiratiebron voor Dantes Inferno in *La Divina Commedia*.

The impressive floor area (ca. 600m²) consists of a succession of smaller blocks and other features: a covered terrace and barbecue, a pool house and space for technical equipment.
The garden is over a hectare in size.

Les impressionnants 600m² de surface habitable proviennent de l'addition d'un certain nombre de bâtiments et annexes plus modestes : une terrasse couverte avec barbecue, une poolhouse et son local technique.
Le jardin couvre plus d'un hectare.

Het aanzienlijke woonoppervlak (ca. 600 m2) wordt bereikt door een opeenvolging van kleinere blokken en bijhorigheden: een overdekt terras met barbecue, een pool house en technische ruimte.
De tuin is meer dan 1 Ha groot.

During the recent renovation, the *mas* was furnished in a resolutely contemporary style: concrete floors, monochrome colours, simple doors and windows and a few carefully selected pieces of designer furniture and ethnic objects.

Lors de la rénovation récente, le mas a été aménagé dans un style résolument contemporain : sols de béton coulé, décoration monochrome, fenêtres et portes austères et quelques meubles design et objets ethniques soigneusement sélectionnés.

Tijdens de recente renovatie werd de mas in een resoluut hedendaagse stijl ingericht: in beton gegoten vloeren, monochrome kleuren, strakke deur- en vensteropeningen en enkele goedgekozen designmeubelen en etnische objecten.

These new wrought-iron windows offer a beautiful view of the garden.

Ces nouveaux châssis de fenêtres, réalisés en fer forgé, offrent une belle vue sur le jardin.

Deze nieuwe ramen, uitgevoerd in smeedijzer, bieden een mooi zicht op de tuin.

Pictures are projected onto the wall in the TV room.

Dans le salon TV, les images sont projetées en direct sur le mur.

In de tv-kamer worden beelden op de muur geprojecteerd.

Simplicity and serenity were key to the design of the dining room and kitchen as well.

Dans la salle à manger et la cuisine, priorité a également été donnée à la sobriété et à la création d'une ambiance sereine.

Ook in de eetkamer en de keuken stonden soberheid en sereniteit centraal.

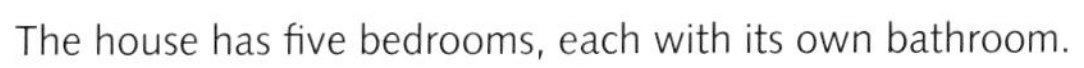

The house has five bedrooms, each with its own bathroom.

La maison compte cinq chambres à coucher, chacune assortie de sa propre salle de bains.

De woning telt vijf slaapkamers met elk hun eigen badkamer.

All of the interior doors and some of the panelling are in rough, horizontal wood planks, creating a streamlined, yet warm atmosphere.

Toutes les portes intérieures et quelques lambrissages sont exécutés à l'aide de planches de bois brut placées à l'horizontale, ce qui confère aux espaces un rayonnement à la fois strict et d'une grande convivialité.

Alle binnendeuren en enkele lambriseringen zijn uitgevoerd in ruwe houten planken die horizontaal geplaatst werden: een strakke en tegelijkertijd toch ook warme uitstraling.

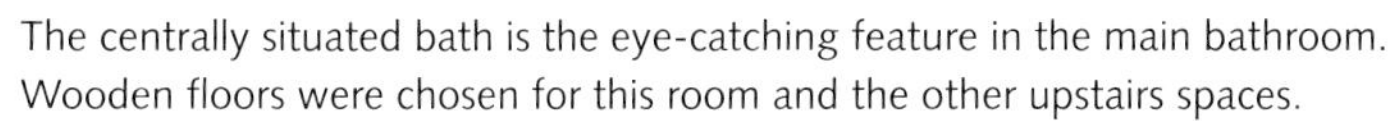

The centrally situated bath is the eye-catching feature in the main bathroom. Wooden floors were chosen for this room and the other upstairs spaces.

Dans la grande salle de bains, la baignoire, placée au centre de la pièce, attire délibérément l'attention. Comme partout à l'étage, les sols sont couverts de planchers de bois.

Het centraal geplaatste bad is de blikvanger in de hoofdbadkamer. Net zoals overal op de bovenverdieping werd hier voor houten vloeren gekozen.

THE ECLECTIC RESTORATION OF AN 18th-CENTURY BASTIDE NEAR AIX

LA RESTAURATION ÉCLECTIQUE D'UNE BASTIDE DU 18e SIÈCLE, À PROXIMITÉ D'AIX-EN-PROVENCE

DE ECLECTISCHE RESTAURATIE VAN EEN XVIIIde-EEUWSE BASTIDE NABIJ AIX

In the immediate surroundings of Aix-en-Provence, you can still find a number of well-preserved,
majestic bastides dating from the seventeenth and eighteenth centuries.
One of these bastides, idyllically situated in a conifer wood, has very recently been completely restored by the current owners.
They chose to restore the eighteenth-century bastide to its former glory, while adding contemporary touches.
This report features an eclectic and harmonious home: contemporary top design in combination with a historic site.
The owners consulted Josselin Fleury from Designer's Studio in Aix-en-Provence: a design boutique and also a studio for interior design.

Dans les environs immédiats d'Aix-en-Provence, il arrive que l'on trouve encore une bastide ou l'autre, majestueuse et en bon état, datant des 17e et 18e siècles.
Une de ces bastides, délicieusement nichée au cœur d'un bois de conifères, a été récemment rénovée en profondeur par ses propriétaires actuels.
Ils ont délibérément opté pour rétablir dans son style d'origine le bâtiment, qui date du 18e, tout en lui ajoutant une solide dose d'art de vivre contemporain.
Ce reportage est donc consacré à un ensemble particulièrement éclectique qui respire néanmoins l'harmonie :
un design contemporain de qualité, intégré dans un cadre historique.
Les maîtres de l'ouvrage ont puisé conseils et inspiration auprès de Josselin Fleury du Designer's Studio d'Aix-en-Provence,
une boutique de design qui se double d'un bureau d'études en aménagements d'intérieurs.

In de nabije omgeving van Aix-en-Provence vindt men nog steeds enkele goed bewaarde
en majestueuze bastides die dateren uit de zeventiende en de achttiende eeuw.
Eén van deze bastides, idyllisch gelegen in een bos van naaldbomen, werd zeer recent volledig gerestaureerd door de huidige eigenaars.
Ze opteerden ervoor om de achttiende-eeuwse bastide in haar vroegere luister te herstellen, maar tegelijkertijd een belangrijke hedendaagse toets aan te brengen.
Deze reportage toont dan ook een uiterst eclectisch maar toch harmonisch geheel: hedendaagse topdesign in combinatie met een historische site.
De opdrachtgevers gingen ten rade bij Josselin Fleury van Designer's Studio in Aix-en-Provence:
een designboetiek en tegelijkertijd ook studiebureau in interieurinrichting.

The facade immediately sets the tone: the charm, sophistication and allure of an eighteenth-century *bastide*, but with contemporary accents. The shutters are in grey/beige lime paints.

La façade avant donne le ton : tout le charme, le raffinement et l'allure d'une bastide du 18e y sont agrémentés d'accents d'aujourd'hui. Les volets ont été peints en gris/beige avec des peintures à base de chaux.

De voorgevel zet meteen de toon: de charme, het raffinement en de allure van een achttiende-eeuwse bastide, maar met hedendaagse accenten. De luiken werden in grijs/beige met kalkverven geschilderd.

A driveway with old plane trees leads to the stately *bastide*.

Une allée d'accès bordée de vieux platanes mène à la noble bastide.

De oprijlaan met oude platanen leidt naar de statige bastide.

The *bastide* is situated in beautiful natural surroundings near Aix-en-Provence. The cypresses separate the house from the conifer woods behind.

La bastide est construite dans un paysage naturel admirable, aux confins d'Aix-en-Provence. Les cyprès soulignent le bâtiment qui se détache sur le bois de conifères à l'arrière-plan.

De bastide is gelegen in een prachtig natuurlandschap in de omgeving van Aix-en-Provence. De cipressen markeren de woning ten opzichte van het achterliggende naaldbos.

The swimming pool is on a lower level, protected from the *mistral*. The loungers with white cushions are from Gandia Blasco, model: Na Xamena (a Ramon Esteve design).

La piscine se situe un peu plus bas, bien à l'abri du mistral. Les lits de repos garnis de coussins blancs sont de Gandia Blasco, modèle Na Xamena (un concept de Ramon Esteve).

Het zwembad is iets lager gelegen, goed beschut tegen de mistral. De loungers met de witte kussens zijn van Gandia Blasco, model Na Xamena (een ontwerp van Ramon Esteve).

The benches and tables are also a creation by Ramon Esteve for Gandia Blasco.

Les banquettes et les tables sont également des créations de Ramon Esteve pour Gandia Blasco.

Ook de banken en tafels zijn een creatie van Ramon Esteve voor Gandia Blasco.

Two white leather sofas B&B Italia amongst family portraits and the owner's collection of wooden aeroplanes.
A Po standing lamp by Capellini.

Deux canapés en cuir blanc de B&B Italia trônent au milieu des portraits de famille et de la collection de modèles réduits d'avions en bois que détient le propriétaire.
Lampe Po de Capellini.

Twee canapés in wit leder van B&B Italia temidden van de familieportretten en de collectie houten vliegtuigjes van de eigenaar. Een staanlamp Po van Capellini.

A marble Venus welcomes the visitor to the former "piano nobile". The old parquet has been retained and bleached.

Une Venus de marbre accueille les visiteurs à l'ancien «étage noble». Le parquet ancien a été restauré et blanchi.

Een marmeren Venus verwelkomt de bezoeker op de voormalige "nobele verdieping". De oude parketvloer werd gerestaureerd en gebleekt.

The Boffi kitchen, the dining room and the sitting room flow together in one large space.
The long dining table was designed by l'Atelier des Remparts in Pertuis. Chairs by Ray and Charles Eames for Vitra. The red-and-yellow-striped chair is a creation by Gaetano Pesce for B&B Italia.

La cuisine Boffi, la salle à manger et le salon ne constituent visuellement qu'un seul grand espace.
La longue table de salle à manger a été dessinée par l'Atelier des Remparts, à Pertuis. Les chaises sont un concept de Ray & Charles Eames, pour Vitra. Le siège rayé de rouge et jaune est une création de Gaetano Pesce pour B&B Italia.

De Boffi keuken, de eetruimte en het salon vloeien in elkaar over in één grote ruimte.
De lange eettafel werd ontworpen door l'Atelier des Remparts in Pertuis. Stoelen ontworpen door Ray en Charles Eames voor Vitra. De rood/geel-gestreepte zetel is een creatie van Gaetano Pesce voor B&B Italia.

Josselin Fleury (Designer's Studio in Aix) suggested a B&B Italia sofa for the sitting room.
The work against the right-hand wall is by the Spanish painter and mixed-media artist Juan Manuel Pajares.

Josselin Fleury (Designer's Studio, à Aix) a proposé d'adopter dans le salon un canapé de B&B Italia.
L'œuvre d'art figurant sur le mur de droite est du peintre et artiste «mixed media» espagnol Juan Manuel Pajares.

Josselin Fleury (Designer's Studio in Aix) stelde in het salon een canapé voor van B&B Italia.
Het werk tegen de rechterwand is van de Spaanse schilder en mixed media kunstenaar Juan Manuel Pajares.

Genuine cinema folding doors in authentic surroundings.

De véritables portes pliantes de cinéma, dans l'environnement d'une authentique salle à l'ancienne.

Echte bioscoop plooideurtjes in een authentiek cinematografische omgeving.

A bedroom in shades of grey-brown and white.
The hanging lamp is by Maxalto, the white drawers are by B&B Italia.

L'ambiance de cette chambre à coucher est conditionnée
par des variations chromatiques qui oscillent
de la couleur gris-brun au blanc.
La lampe à suspension est de Maxalto.
La commode blanche est de B&B Italia.

Deze slaapkamer baadt in de grijsbruine en witte tinten.
De hanglamp is van Maxalto, de witte commode van B&B Italia.

The original frescos were retained in this bathroom. The bath is a design by Philippe Starck for Duravit.

Les fresques d'origine ont été maintenues dans cette salle de bains. La baignoire a été dessinée par Philippe Starck pour Duravit.

De originele fresco's werden behouden in deze badkamer. Het bad is een ontwerp van Philippe Starck voor Duravit.

The dressing room of the lady of the house with a Cappellini chair (design: Patrick Norguet) in a fabric by Pucci. The carpet is a creation by Paola Lenti.

Le dressing de la maîtresse de maison comporte une chaise de Cappellini (design Patrick Norguet), couverte d'un tissu de Pucci. Le tapis est une création de Paola Lenti.

De dressing van de dame des huizes met een stoel van Cappellini (ontwerp Patrick Norguet) bekleed met een stof van Pucci. Het tapijt is een creatie van Paola Lenti.

The dressing room of the gentleman of the house.

Le dressing du maître de maison.

De dressing van de heer des huizes.

A low unit designed and created by l'Atelier des Remparts forms the end of the bed.

La tête de lit de la chambre à coucher principale est constituée d'un meuble bas dessiné et réalisé par l'Atelier des Remparts.

Het bedeinde van de hoofdslaapkamer wordt gevormd door een laag meubel, ontworpen en gerealiseerd door l'Atelier des Remparts.

The bathroom of the lady of the house, with a Boffi bath in the centre.

La salle de bains de madame avec, en son centre, une baignoire de Boffi.

De badkamer van mevrouw met centraal een bad van Boffi.

The children's bedrooms and bathrooms are very contemporary in style, with fresh and cheerful colours.

Les chambres à coucher et salles de bains des enfants sont traitées dans un style résolument contemporain, avec des couleurs tout en fraîcheur et en vivacité.

De kinderslaap- en badkamers zijn resoluut hedendaags, met frisse en opwekkende kleuren.

In spite of the owners' passion for contemporary design, the historic character of this eighteenth-century *bastide* always shines through. The mixture of old and new results in a very eclectic, yet harmonious whole.

Malgré la passion que vouent les habitants au design contemporain, le caractère historique de cette bastide du 18e siècle n'a jamais été trahi. Le mélange de l'ancien et du moderne apparaît certes comme très éclectique, mais reste toujours harmonieux.

Ondanks de passie voor hedendaags design van de bewoners, wordt het historische karakter van deze achttiende-eeuwse bastide nooit verloochend. De mix van oud en nieuw toont een zeer eclectisch en toch harmonieus geheel.

A RENOVATED HOLIDAY HOME BESIDE THE BAY OF SAINT-TROPEZ

UNE VILLA DE VACANCES RÉNOVÉE, SUR LA BAIE DE SAINT-TROPEZ

EEN GERENOVEERDE VAKANTIEVILLA AAN DE BAAI VAN SAINT-TROPEZ

This villa beside the bay of Saint-Tropez was designed in 1950 by architect Raymond Louis, who was also a leading designer;
his creations included the Coca Cola bottle and the Shell logo.
In recent years, this beautifully situated holiday home has been renovated and extended by Belgian architect Michel Lesot from Arquennes.
Gilles de Meulemeester (Ebony Interiors) was responsible for the interior design; the kitchen is a creation by Zen Design from Saint-Tropez.

Cette villa sur la Baie de Saint-Tropez a été dessinée en 1950 par l'architecte Raymond Louis, également très réputé en tant que designer.
C'est lui, notamment, qui a dessiné la bouteille de Coca-Cola et le logo de Shell.
Ces dernières années, cette maison de vacances superbement située a été transformée et agrandie par les soins de l'architecte belge Michel Lesot, originaire d'Arquennes. Gilles de Meulemeester (Ebony Interiors) s'est chargé de l'aménagement intérieur. La cuisine est une réalisation de Zen Design, à Saint-Tropez.

Deze villa aan de baai van Saint-Tropez werd in 1950 ontworpen door architect Raymond Louis, die ook als designer furore maakte:
hij ontwierp o.a. het Coca Cola flesje en het logo van Shell.
De voorbije jaren werd deze prachtig gelegen vakantiewoning verbouwd en uitgebreid door de Belgische architect Michel Lesot uit Arquennes.
Gilles de Meulemeester (Ebony Interiors) verzorgde de interieurinrichting, de keuken is een realisatie van Zen Design uit Saint-Tropez.

The teakwood stairs were added during the recent renovation.

L'escalier en bois de teck a été ajouté lors de la récente rénovation.

De teakhouten trap werd bij de recente verbouwing toegevoegd.

Rather than a typical Provençal fountain in white stone, a more contemporary version in lavastone was chosen for this property.

En lieu et place de la fontaine provençale typique en pierre blanche, on a opté ici pour une variante contemporaine en pierre de lave.

In plaats van de typische Provençaalse fonteiten in witsteen, werd hier geopteerd voor een hedendaagsere variant in lavasteen.

The large teakwood terraces provide a constantly changing view of the bay.

Les vastes terrasses en bois de teck donnent sur la baie une vue sans cesse changeante.

De ruime terrassen in teakhout kijken uit op het steeds veranderende zicht op de baai.

A beige natural stone, Antalya cream, has been used for the living areas. Red combined with beige is the main colour scheme throughout the property.

Dans toutes les pièces à vivre, on a choisi d'installer de la pierre naturelle beige Antalya Cream. En combinaison avec le beige, le rouge est la couleur dominante qui a été sélectionnée pour le décor de l'ensemble de la maison.

In alle dagvertrekken werd een beige natuursteen, Antalya Cream geplaatst. In combinatie met beige is rood het hoofdmotief in de kleurenkeuze van de hele vakantiewoning.

The Moroccan vases were supplied by Ebony.

Les vases marocains ont été fournis par Ebony.

De Marokkaanse vazen werden door Ebony geleverd.

The sofas with their white cotton covers are by Tacchini. All of the throws and cushions were supplied by Ebony, as were the coffee table (Artelano) and the standing lamps (by Modénature).

Les canapés couverts de coton blanc font partie de la collection Tacchini. Tous les plaids et coussins ont été fournis par Ebony, ainsi que la table de salon (Artelano) et les lampadaires (Modénature).

De met witte katoen beklede canapés zijn van Tacchini. Alle plaids en kussens werden door Ebony geleverd, evenals de salontafel (Artelano) en de staanlampen (van Modénature).

The kitchen is a creation by Zen Design from Saint-Tropez.

La cuisine est un concept de Zen Design, à Saint-Tropez.

De keuken is een ontwerp van Zen Design uit Saint-Tropez.

The fuchsia work of art in the background is by Michel Mouffe.

L'œuvre d'art fuchsia figurant à l'arrière-plan est de Michel Mouffe.

Het fuchsia kunstwerk op de achtergrond is van Michel Mouffe.

The chairs, benches and hanging lamps were specially designed by Ebony.

Les chaises, les banquettes et les lampes ont été confectionnées sur mesure par Ebony.

De stoelen, banken en de hanglampen werden door Ebony op maat gemaakt.

The red barstools were created by designer duo Bataille + ibens.

Les tabourets de bar rouges ont été dessinés par le duo de designers Bataille + ibens.

De rode barkrukken werden ontworpen door het designerduo Bataille + ibens.

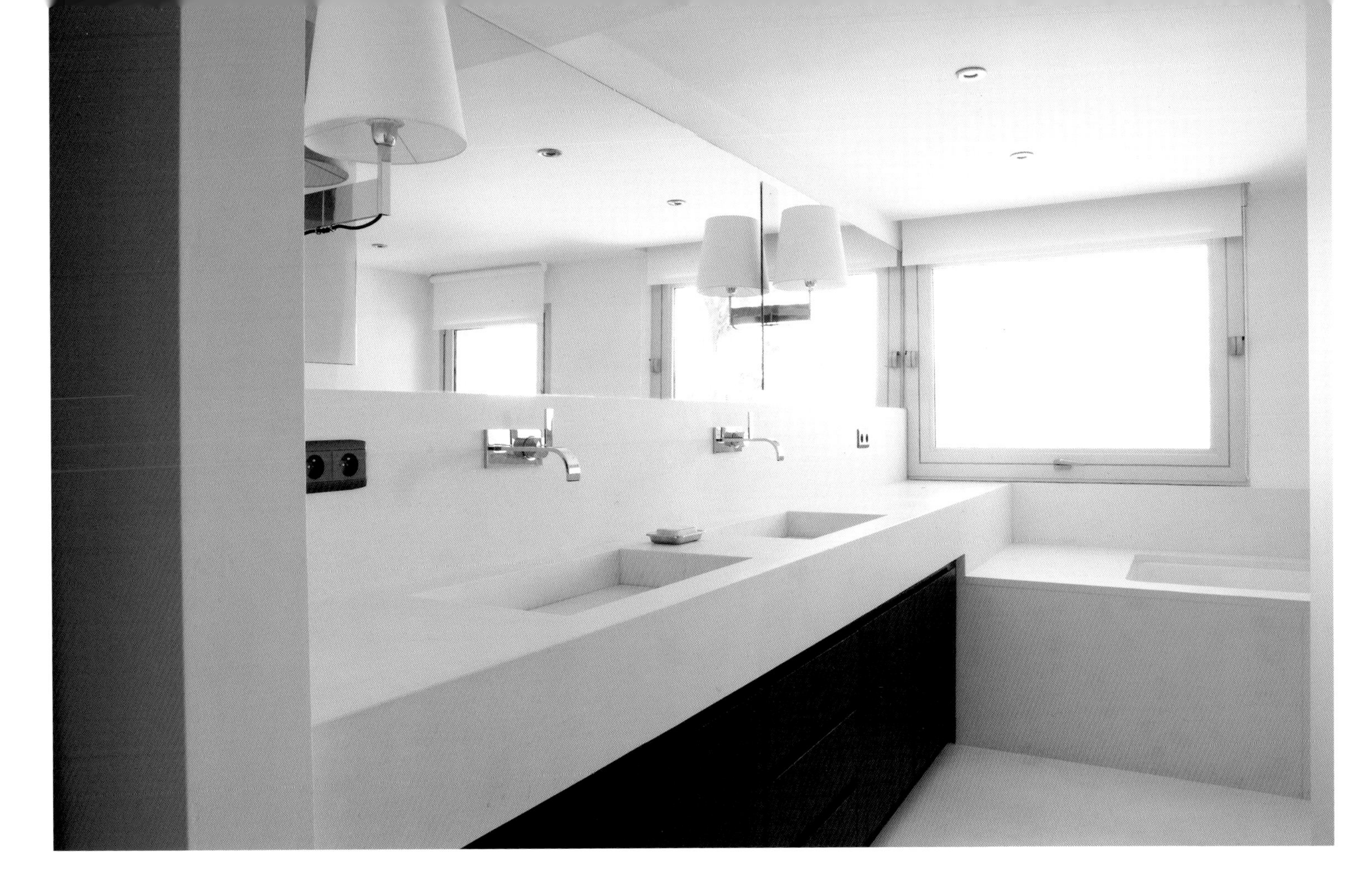

Antalya cream natural stone in the bathroom too.
Wall lamps by Liaigre; taps by Dornbracht.

Dans la salle de bains également, on a fait usage de la pierre naturelle Antalya Cream.
Lampes murales de Liaigre. Robinetterie de Dornbracht.

Ook in de badkamer werd Antalya Cream natuursteen gebruikt.
Wandlampen van Liaigre, kraanwerk Dornbracht.

Another wonderful view from this bedroom window with its linen blinds.
Oak parquet for the floor.

Un paysage captivant, au départ de cette chambre à coucher équipée de stores en lin.
Ici, le sol est revêtu d'un parquet de chêne.

Een prachtig zicht ook vanuit deze slaapkamer met linnen stores.
Als vloerbekleding werd hier voor een eiken parket gekozen.

An oak headboard in harmony with the painted wall behind the bed.

La tête de lit est exécutée en chêne, de telle sorte qu'elle s'harmonise avec le mur peint, derrière le lit.

Het hoofdeinde is in eiken uitgevoerd, in harmonie met de geschilderde wand achter het bed.

The shower is in Cotto d'Este tiles.

La douche est garnie de carreaux Cotto d'Este.

De douche werd met Cotto d'Este tegels bekleed.

More playful pastel and orange shades in the other bedrooms. In contrast, the bathrooms are simple and almost monochrome.

Des variations chromatiques vives, en tons pastel et orange, dominent dans les autres chambres à coucher. Par contraste, les salles de bains sont sobres et pratiquement monochromes.

Speelsere pastel- en oranje tinten in de andere slaapkamers. De badkamers zijn daarentegen strak en quasi monochroom.

AN UNDERSTATED HOLIDAY HOME IN RAMATUELLE

UNE MAISON DE VACANCES DISCRÈTE À RAMATUELLE

EEN INGETOGEN VAKANTIEHUIS IN RAMATUELLE

Christel De Vos (De Vos Projects) created this newly built villa in Ramatuelle, in collaboration with Nathalie Mousny.
The house was given a stucco finish and painted white; only the roof tiles reveal a Provençal inspiration.

Christel De Vos (De Vos Projects) a réalisé en collaboration avec Nathalie Mousny une nouvelle villa à Ramatuelle.
Toute la maison a été stuquée et peinte ensuite en blanc. Seules les tuiles font encore référence à une inspiration provençale.

Christel De Vos (De Vos Projects) realiseerde in samenwerking met Nathalie Mousny een nieuwbouwvilla in Ramatuelle.
Het volledige huis werd gestuct en vervolgens wit geschilderd ; enkel de dakpannen verwijzen nog naar Provençaalse inspiratie.

The driveway is in concrete. The old parasol trees were already present.
The lights are a creation by De Vos Projects. Zzip carried out the lighting study and coordination.
The antique bench is from Indonesia.

L'allée d'accès a été bétonnée. Les vieux pins parasols étaient présents de longue date sur le terrain.
Les lampes sont une création de De Vos Projects. L'étude et la coordination de l'ensemble des éclairages ont été réalisées par Zzip.
Le banc ancien est d'origine indonésienne.

De oprit werd gebetonneerd. De oude parasolbomen waren al op het terrein aanwezig.
De lampen zijn een creatie van De Vos Projects. De volledige lichtstudie en –coördinatie gebeurde door Zzip.
De antieke bank is uit Indonesië afkomstig.

The laurel hedge is an evergreen. The entrance door is finished in black paint.

La haie en lauriers reste verte en hiver. La porte d'entrée a été peinte en noir.

De haag in laurier is wintergroen. De inkomdeur werd zwart geschilderd.

All of the terraces and the interior floors are in a French castle stone, Abbaye Castilla.
The ancient olive tree was brought in as a new feature.
Cane chairs and table by Manutti.

Toutes les terrasses et les sols intérieurs ont été réalisés en un dallage de château français, Abbaye Castilla.
L'olivier séculaire a été importé.
Chaises de rotin et table de Manutti.

Alle terrassen en de binnenvloeren werden in een Franse kasteelvloer, Abbaye Castilla, uitgevoerd.
De eeuwenoude olijfboom werd ingevoerd.
Rieten stoelen en tafel van Manutti.

Antheunis supplied the swimming pool equipment and the Bisazza glass mosaic for the lining.
The white garden chairs and table are by Tribu. The stone was found in a local quarry.

Les appareillages techniques de la piscine et son recouvrement en mosaïques de verre Bisazza ont été assurés par Antheunis.
Les chaises blanches et la table de jardin viennent de chez Tribu. Les moellons ont été découverts dans une carrière locale.

De zwembadtechnieken en de Bisazza-glasmozaïek binnenbekleding werden door Antheunis verzorgd.
De witte tuinstoelen en tafel zijn van Tribu. De breuksteen werd in een lokale groeve gevonden.

COOL RESTAURANTS
LUXURY HOTELS

The pale beige Abbaye Castilla natural stone creates a feeling of warmth and serenity in every room. The table is one of Christel De Vos's own designs. Sofas by Meridiani in white cotton.

Le recours à la pierre naturelle beige clair Abbaye Castilla confère à chaque pièce une ambiance chaleureuse et sereine. La table est une création de Christel De Vos elle-même. Les canapés en coton blanc sont de Meridiani.

De zachtbeige Abbaye Castilla natuursteen zorgt voor warmte en sereniteit in elke ruimte. De tafel is een eigen ontwerp van Christel De Vos. Canapés van Meridiani in wit katoen.

The Bulthaup kitchen with Botticino work surface and stools designed by Bataille + ibens.

La cuisine Bulthaup est équipée de plans de travail en Botticino et de tabourets dessinés par Bataille + ibens.

De Bulthaup keuken met werkbladen in Botticino en krukken ontworpen door Bataille + ibens.

The dining-room chairs are by Meridiani.

Les chaises de salle à manger sont de Meridiani.

De eetkamerstoelen zijn van Meridiani.

Egemin-ECS coordinated the integral electricity, home-automation and air-cooling systems. The floors can be cooled.

Les travaux d'installation de l'électricité, de la domotique et de la climatisation ont été coordonnés par Egemin-ECS. Les sols peuvent être rafraîchis.

De integrale electriciteits-, domotica- en luchtkoelingswerken werden door Egemin-ECS gecoördineerd. De vloeren kunnen gekoeld worden.

The white painted Jasno shutters filter out the bright sunlight.

Les stores Jasno peints en blanc filtrent la lumière vive du soleil.

De witgeschilderde Jasno shutters filteren het felle zonlicht.

The bathroom floor is also in Abbaye Castilla tiles, but the washbasins and bath surround are in Italian Botticino marble.

Le sol de la salle de bains est pavé, lui aussi, de carrelages Abbaye Castilla, alors que les lavabos et l'habillage de la baignoire sont en marbre italien Botticino.

De badkamervloer is eveneens in Abbaye Castilla tegels, maar de wastafels en de badbekleding zijn in Italiaanse Botticino marmer uitgevoerd.

Christel De Vos also designed all of the bedrooms. She found the headboard in an antiques shop.

Toutes les chambres à coucher ont également été dessinées par Christel De Vos. Elle a trouvé la tête de lit chez un antiquaire.

Alle slaapkamers werden eveneens door Christel De Vos ontworpen. Het beddehoofd vond ze bij een antiquair.

A MODERNIST RETREAT IN THE CÔTE D'AZUR

UN REFUGE MODERNISTE SUR LA CÔTE D'AZUR

EEN MODERNISTISCH BUITENVERBLIJF AAN DE CÔTE D'AZUR

A faux-Provencal farmhouse was completely stripped of all folksy detailing and transformed
into a calming modernist refuge by the architectural office Kallos – Turin.
The interior was gutted to create an open, double-height living space at the heart of the plan that opens directly to the exterior pool terrace.
An infinity edge pool acts as the boundary to the terrace with drops steeply at the view edge making the site feel simultaneously expansive and private.
Large monolithic slabs of amber-hued Palladian limestone flow seamlessly through the main living spaces and to the exterior,
blurring the boundary between inside and out. The limestone becomes a theme in the house monolithically wrapping stairs,
counters and walls and filling the space with a honey-toned light. The project combines a relaxed atmosphere with precise detailing.

Cette ferme de faux style provençal a été entièrement épurée de ses accessoires traditionnels
et a été transformée par le bureau d'architecture Kallos – Turin, en un refuge moderniste tout en tranquillité.
L'intérieur a été vidé en vue de créer un lieu de vie ouvert à deux niveaux, au cœur d'un espace qui ouvre directement sur la terrasse extérieure et la piscine.
La piscine à débordement met un terme à la terrasse et donne lieu à un à pic qui ouvre l'horizon et confère au site une dimension à la fois illimitée et privative.
De grandes dalles monolithiques de pierre calcaire ambrée palladienne couvrent d'une façon continue les principaux espaces à vivre et se prolongent en extérieur,
effaçant la limite entre intérieur et extérieur. La pierre calcaire est considérée comme un thème permanent dans cette maison.
Elle habille de façon monolithique les escaliers, les volumes et les murs, et meuble l'espace d'une lumière aux accents de miel.
Le projet table sur une combinaison entre des ambiances tout en tranquillité et une grande attention portée aux détails.

Een faux-Provençal hoeve werd volledig ontdaan van al zijn traditionele details
en door het architectenbureau Kallos – Turin omgevormd tot een rustgevend modernistisch toevluchtsoord.
De binnenkant werd volledig opengebroken, waardoor in het centrum van de hoeve een open en dubbelhoge leefruimte ontstond die direct uitgeeft op het buitenterras met zwembad. Een overloopzwembad grenst het terras af dat steil naar beneden loopt waardoor het zicht oneindig lijkt en waardoor de plek tegelijk enorm uitgestrekt en privé aanvoelt. Grote monolitische platen van amberkleurige Palladiaanse kalksteen lopen naadloos doorheen de belangrijkste leefruimtes en naar buiten toe, waardoor de grens tussen binnen en buiten vervaagt. Kalksteen wordt een van de thema's in het huis. Zowel trappen en werkbladen als muren zijn gemaakt van deze monolitische stenen en vervullen de ruimte met een honingkleurig licht. Het project combineert een ontspannen sfeer met precieze details.

The infinity edge pool accentuates the drop off to the site.

La piscine à débordement accentue l'ouverture visuelle vers le paysage.

Het overloopzwembad accentueert de steile rand van de site.

The pool terrace is the extension of the interior spaces.

La terrasse de la piscine agit comme une extension des espaces intérieurs.

Het terras met zwembad ligt in het verlengde van de binnenruimtes.

The dining terrace which is an extension of the kitchen has views over the pool and to the landscape beyond.

La terrasse à dîner est une forme d'extension de la cuisine. Elle ouvre la vue sur la piscine et sur le paysage environnant.

Het eetterras ligt in het verlengde van de keuken en kijkt uit over het zwembad en het landschap erachter.

View from the dining terrace.

Vue de la terrasse à dîner.

Zicht vanop het eetterras.

The 3 m long exterior dining table was carved from a solid piece of stone and craned into position.

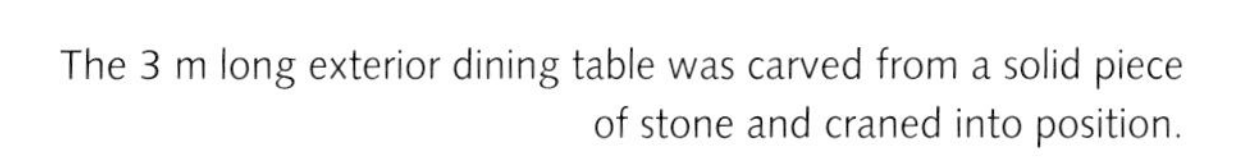

La table de salle à manger extérieure de 3m de long a été taillée dans un bloc de pierre et a été mise en place à l'aide d'une grue.

De 3 m lange buiteneettafel werd uit een massief stuk steen gehouwen en in de juiste positie gehesen.

Precise detailing and expert installation by Italian stonemasons allows the stone to read as a solid carved block.

L'attention portée aux détails et une installation experte par un maçon italien expérimenté donnent l'illusion qu'il s'agit d'un monolithe de pierre.

De precieze decoratie en deskundige installering door Italiaanse steenhouwers zorgen ervoor dat de steen er staat als een massieve gehouwen blok.

A monolithic stone stair leads from the entry platform to the office and master suite.

Un escalier de pierre monolithique mène de la plate-forme d'entrée vers le bureau et les appartements principaux.

Een trap uit monolitische steen leidt van het platform aan de ingang naar de studeerkamer en de suite van de eigenaars.

Light sources are subtly concealed under benches and below stairs.

Les sources de lumières sont subtilement dissimulées sous les banquettes et en bas des escaliers.

Lichtbronnen worden subtiel verborgen achter zitbanken en onder trappen.

Silk laminated glass panels enclose the office mezzanine and emit an amber glow.

Des panneaux de verre laminé soyeux entourent le bureau en mezzanine et émettent des reflets ambrés.

Panelen van gelamineerd glas met zijdeglans sluiten de kantoormezzanine af en stralen een amberkleurige gloed uit.

The crispness of the architectural detailing is countered by a loosely draped crystal chandelier.

Le caractère strict du détail architectural est édulcoré par un lustre de cristal élégamment drapé.

De zin voor het strikt architecturale detail staat in schril contract met de zichtbaar nonchalante kristallen kroonluchter.

The white lacquer clad kitchen links the living space and the dining terrace.

La cuisine habillée de laque blanche côtoie l'espace à vivre et la terrasse à dîner.

De witgelakte keuken verbindt de leefruimte met het eetterras.

A monochromatic and homogeneous use of materials and color was the key to creating a warm and calming environment. Emphasis is on the warmth of the natural light in that part of France.

Une utilisation monochrome et homogène des matériaux et des coloris a permis de créer des ambiances chaudes et apaisantes. L'emphase a été mise sur la sauvegarde du caractère chaleureux de la lumière naturelle, dans cette région de France.

Het monochromatisch en homogeen gebruik van materialen en kleuren was cruciaal voor het creëren van een warme en rustgevende omgeving. De nadruk ligt op de warmte van het daglicht in dat deel van Frankrijk.

The bathrooms are wrapped in amber toned limestone to accentuate the warm soft light to the area.

Les salles de bains sont habillées de pierres calcaires aux reflets ambrés qui accentuent la douceur et la chaleur de la lumière ambiante.

De badkamers zijn ontworpen in amberkleurige kalksteen om het warme zachte licht te accentueren in de ruimte.

A brightly coloured Perspex chair offsets the buttery tones of the master bedroom.

Une chaise en Perspex de couleurs vives tranche sur les teintes crémeuses de la chambre à coucher principale.

Een bonte Perspex-stoel compenseert de boterkleurige tinten in de slaapkamer van de eigenaars.

A MODERN RESIDENTIAL BLOCK
WITH A BREATHTAKING SEA VIEW

UN "BLOC À VIVRE" CONTEMPORAIN
AVEC UNE FASCINANTE VUE SUR MER

EEN HEDENDAAGSE WOONDOOS
MET ADEMBENEMEND ZEEZICHT

Collection Privée is a renowned interior-design store with branches in Cannes and Valbonne.
The company also has a studio for architecture and interior design, headed by Gilles Pellerin and Nicolette Schouten.
The project in this report is the architectural studio's most recent creation on the Côte d'Azur:
a defiantly contemporary variant on the Provençal villa.
Geometric shapes, symmetry and balance are the key to this simply designed block.

Société renommée dans l'univers de l'ameublement, Collection Privée est établie à Cannes et à Valbonne.
L'entreprise possède également un bureau d'études en architecture et en aménagement d'intérieurs, dirigé par Gilles Pellerin et Nicolette Schouten.
Le projet que présente ce reportage est la réalisation la plus récente du bureau d'architecture :
une déclinaison résolument contemporaine de la villa provençale typique, sur la Côte d'Azur.
Des formes géométriques et symétriques constituent la base de l'équilibre de ce "bloc à vivre" dessiné dans un style très strict.

Collection Privée is een gerenommeerde interieurzaak met vestigingen in Cannes en Valbonne.
Daarnaast heeft het bedrijf ook een studiebureau voor architectuur en interieurinrichting, geleid door Gilles Pellerin en Nicolette Schouten.
Het project in deze reportage is de meest recente realisatie aan de Azurenkust van het architectenbureau:
een resoluut hedendaagse variant op de Provençaalse villa.
Geometrische vormen, symmetrie en evenwicht staan centraal in deze strak vormgegeven "woondoos".

Parts of the exterior walls are painted white, but some is in rough gneiss stone.

Les façades ont été en grande partie peintes en blanc, mais une partie en est exécutée en pierre Gneiss brute.

De gevels werden gedeeltelijk wit geschilderd, maar een deel is in ruwe Gneiss-steen uitgevoerd.

A contemporary interpretation of the Provençal "restanques", low walls that harmoniously integrate the different levels.

Une interprétation contemporaine des "restanques" provençales, ces murettes basses qui intègrent harmonieusement les différences de niveaux.

Een hedendaagse interpretatie van de Provençaalse "restanques", de lage muurtjes die niveauverschillen harmonisch integreren.

The terraces are in Italian Pietra Serena natural stone.

Les terrasses sont couvertes de pierres naturelles italiennes Pietra Serena.

De terrassen zijn met Italiaanse Pietra Serena natuursteen bekleed.

Teakwood was chosen for around the swimming pool. The infinity swimming pool is in stone mosaic tiles.

Pour les contours de la piscine, on a opté pour le bois de teck. La piscine affleurante est entièrement couverte de mosaïques de pierre naturelle.

Rond het zwembad werd voor teakhout geopteerd. Het overlooopzwembad is volledig met natuursteenmozaïek bekleed.

The entrance door is in zinc.

La porte d'entrée est réalisée en zinc.

De inkomdeur is in zink uitgevoerd.

Sofas and coffee tables are by Baltus (Collection Privée). A Flexform armchair.

Les canapés et la table de salon sont des créations de Baltus (chez Collection Privée). Le fauteuil est un Flexform.

Canapés en salontafel zijn van Baltus (bij Collection Privée). De fauteuil is van Flexform.

The kitchen work surface is in Corian. Custom-built oak kitchen units.

Le plan de travail de la cuisine est exécuté en Corian. Confectionné sur mesure, le mobilier de cuisine en chêne a été grisé.

Het keukenwerkblad is in Corian uitgevoerd. De op maat gemaakte keukenmeubelen in eiken werden vergrijsd.

The main bathroom is in a combination of Palmyra natural stone and an oak parquet floor (by Cabuy).

La salle de bains principale marie la pierre naturelle de Palmyre avec un parquet en chêne (de Cabuy).

De hoofdbadkamer bestaat uit een combinatie van Palmyra natuursteen met een eiken parketvloer (door Cabuy).

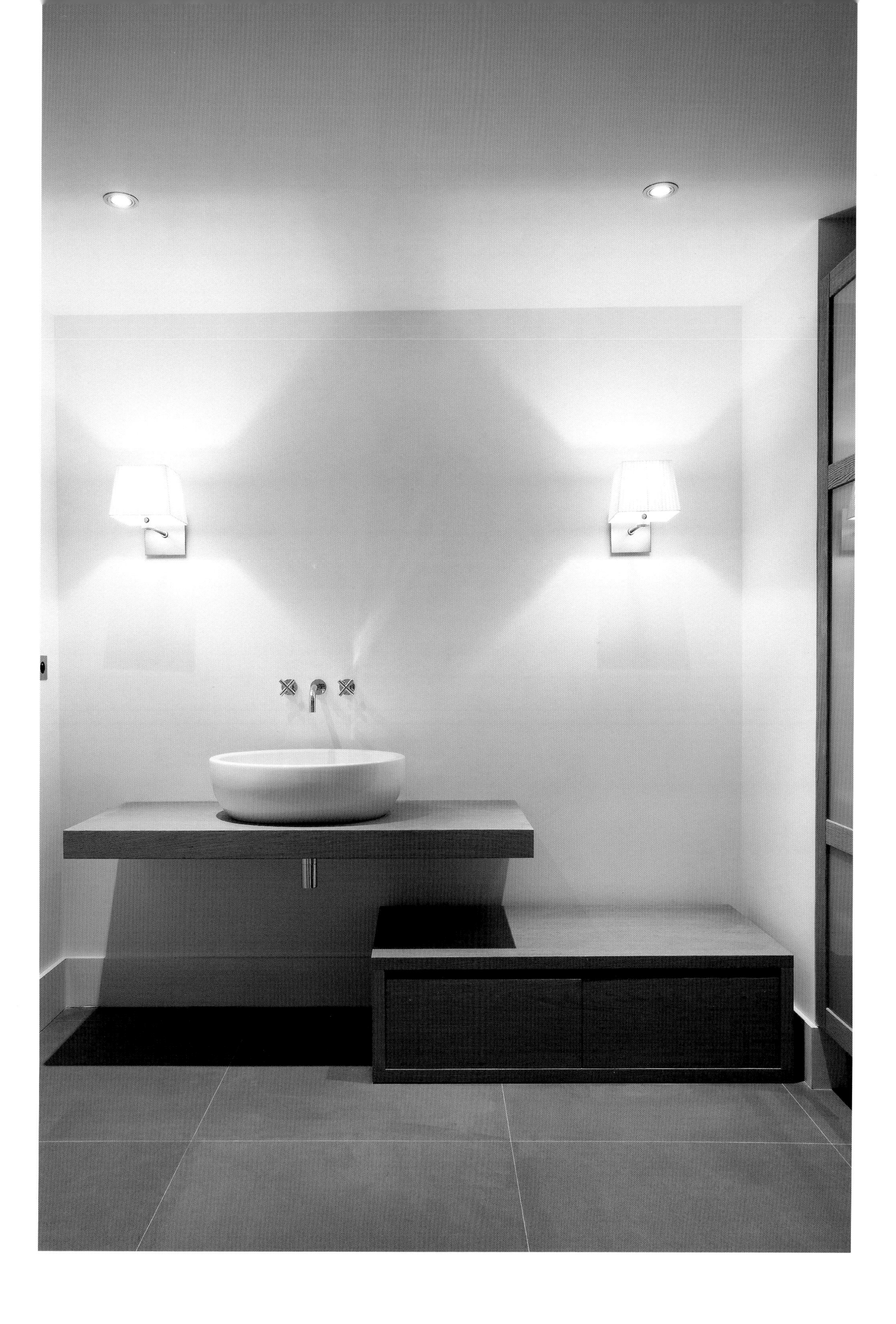

CONTEMPORARY AXES AND PERSPECTIVES IN THE MASSIF DES MAURES

AXES ET PERSPECTIVES CONTEMPORAINES DANS LE MASSIF DES MAURES

HEDENDAAGSE ASSEN EN PERSPECTIEVEN IN HET MASSIEF VAN DE MAURES

Architect Marc Lust did not restrict himself to simply designing this project.
He also put his own work on the backburner for three years to carry out the project himself.
This property, situated in the Massif des Maures, between Hyères and Fréjus,
is a perfect expression of his outlook on contemporary architecture.
This is characterised by a clearly defined network of axes and perspectives
and by the use of light as a fundamental element in the creation of a streamlined and chic space.

L'architecte Marc Lust ne s'est pas contenté de dessiner ce projet,
il a également mis son activité professionnelle entre parenthèses pendant trois ans pour le réaliser de ses mains.
Située dans le massif des Maures, une petite chaîne de montagne entre Hyères et Fréjus (Var),
cette propriété reflète sa conception de l'architecture contemporaine se caractérisant par une rigueur
dans le tracé des axes et perspectives et l'utilisation de la lumière
en tant qu'élément fondamental à la création d'un espace épuré et classieux.

Architect Marc Lust beperkte zich niet tot het ontwerp van dit project.
Hij heeft ook zijn eigen beroepsactiviteiten drie jaar lang op een laag pitje gezet om het project zelf uit te voeren.
Deze eigendom, gelegen in het massief van de Maures, tussen Hyères en Fréjus (Var),
drukt perfect zijn opvatting over de hedendaagse architectuur uit.
Die wordt gekenmerkt door een streng tracé van assen en perspectieven en het gebruik
van licht als fundamenteel element bij het scheppen van een uitgezuiverde en chique ruimte.

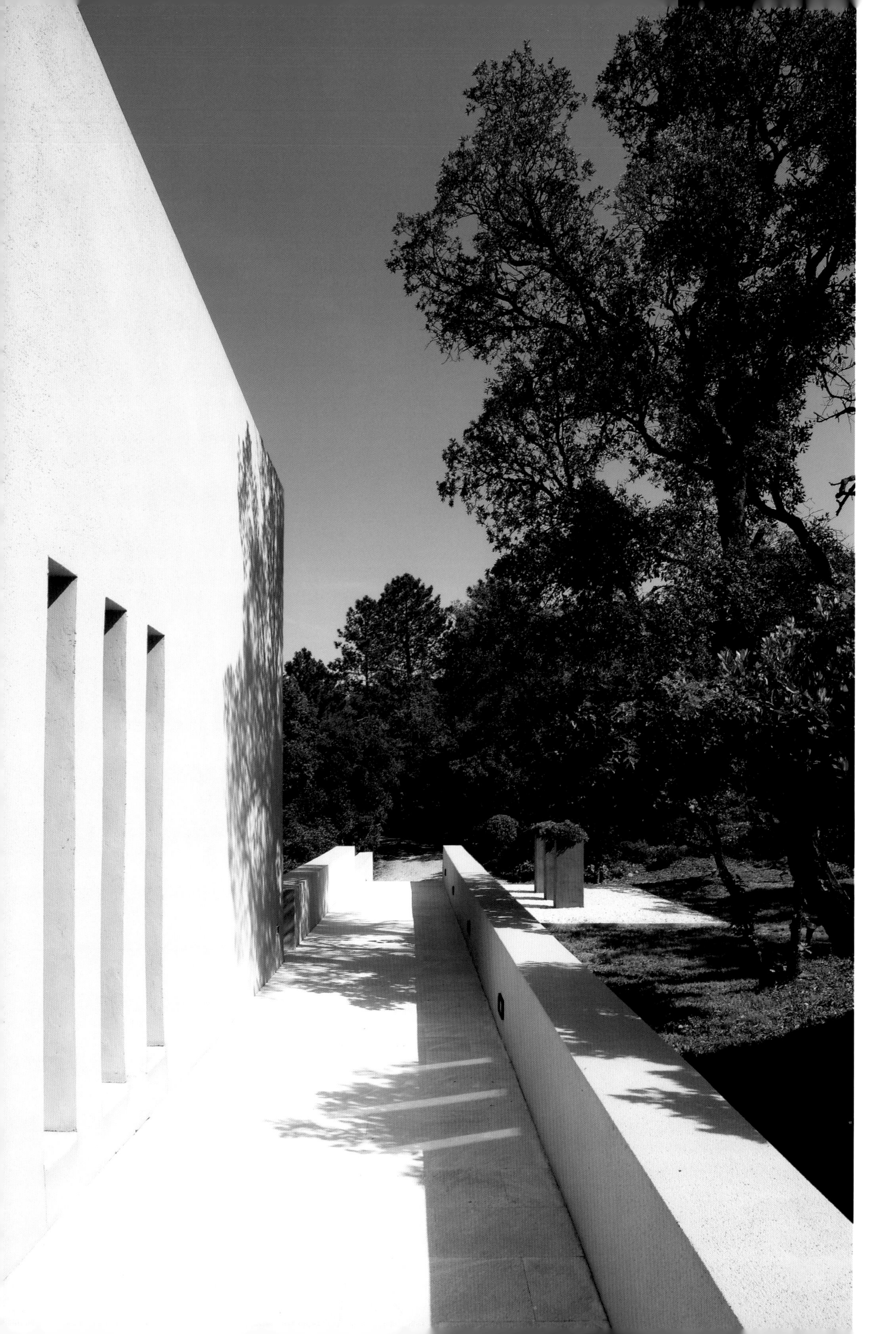

An axis of 25 metres leads to the main entrance. Oak double doors open onto a central patio. The main rooms of the house are situated around the patio.

Un axe de 25 mètres de long mène à l'entrée principale. Après avoir franchi une double porte en chêne, l'on découvre un patio central à ciel ouvert autour duquel s'articulent les pièces principales de la maison.

Een as van 25 meter lang leidt naar de hoofdingang. Via een dubbele eiken deur wordt een centrale patio bereikt – in de openlucht. Rondom de patio liggen de voornaamste kamers van het huis.

The central patio shelters a two-hundred-year-old olive tree and two pools with a waterfall. The transparent glass sections around the patio allow a perfect view of the living area and also highlight the architectural work, which is based upon the interplay of transversal axes and views throughout the property.

Le patio central accueille en son sein un olivier bicentenaire et deux plans d'eau avec cascade. La transparence des baies vitrées qui l'encadrent permet non seulement de découvrir les espaces de vie mais souligne également le travail architectural effectué au niveau des vues et des axes transversaux.

De centrale patio biedt onderdak aan een tweehonderdjarige olijfboom en twee watervlakken met waterval. Door de transparante glaspartijen rondom de patio zijn niet alleen de leefruimten optimaal zichtbaar, maar wordt ook het architecturale werk dat op het vlak van de perspectieven en transversale assen uitgevoerd werd, in de verf gezet.

The terrace area, distributed over different levels, connects the house to the swimming pool. The pool house – with a sun terrace and covered barbecue area – complements the design of the space surrounding the swimming pool. The use of natural stone, teak and white pebbles clearly delineates the entrance and relaxation zones. Stretched tent-cloth provides shade and lends a light-hearted touch.

Le jeu de terrasses, sur différents niveaux, relie la maison à la piscine. Le pool house avec sa terrasse solarium et l'espace barbecue couvert complètent l'aménagement des abords immédiats de la piscine. Le recours à la pierre naturelle, le teck et le gravier blanc délimite les zones d'accès et les plages de repos. Un jeu de toiles tendues apporte ombre et légèreté.

De terraszone, over verschillende niveaus verdeeld, verbindt het huis met het zwembad. Het poolhouse – met zonneterras en overdekte barbecuezone – vervolledigt de inrichting van de omtrek van het zwembad. Door het gebruik van natuursteen, teak en witte kiezelsteen worden de toegangs- en rustzones nauwkeurig afgebakend. Strakgespannen tentzeilen zorgen voor schaduw en een frivole look.

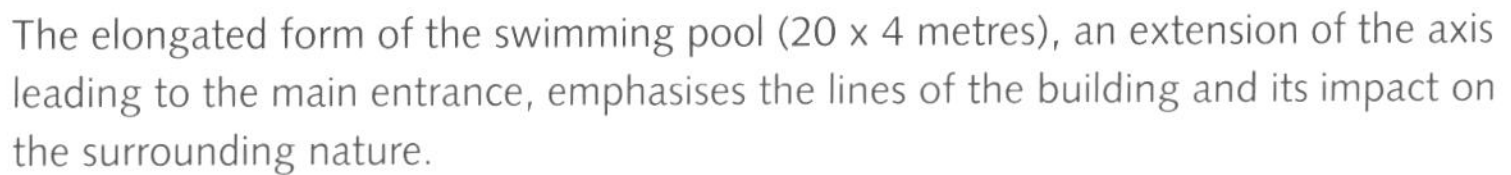

The elongated form of the swimming pool (20 x 4 metres), an extension of the axis leading to the main entrance, emphasises the lines of the building and its impact on the surrounding nature.
The existing Mediterranean vegetation, trimmed into spheres, creates the impression that the architectural project has not imposed itself, but that the natural environment has incorporated it.

Un couloir de nage de 20 x 4 m, situé en prolongation de l'axe d'accès menant à l'entrée principale, accentue, par sa longueur, l'ampleur de l'oeuvre et son emprise dans la nature environnante.
La végétation méditerranéenne existante, par une taille en boules, donne à penser que le projet architectural ne s'est pas imposé au lieu mais plutôt que la nature l'a intégré en son sein.

Een zwemgang van 20 x 4 m, gelegen in het verlengde van de toegangsas die naar de hoofdingang leidt, beklemtoont, door zijn langwerpige vorm, de uitstraling van het bouwwerk en zijn impact op de natuur.
De bestaande mediterrane vegetatie – gesnoeid in bolvorm – doet vermoeden dat het architecturale project zich niet opgedrongen heeft, maar dat de natuur het als het ware geïntegreerd heeft.

The high ceilings, the white walls and the tiled floor in pale natural stone contribute to the feeling of calm in this place. The spacious sitting room opens onto the patio on one side and the swimming pool on the other side, via large glass windows. The suspended fireplace wall also serves as a projection screen. The interior design, by Joëlle Lust, is chic and sophisticated, streamlined, yet not plain.

Les hauts plafonds, les murs blancs et le sol en grandes dalles de pierre naturelle claire participent à la quiétude des lieux. Le vaste salon s'ouvre d'un côté sur le patio et de l'autre, par de grandes baies vitrées en galandage, sur la piscine. La paroi suspendue de la cheminée sert également d'écran de projection. L'aménagement intérieur, réalisé par Joëlle Lust, se veut chic et raffiné, épuré mais sans austérité.

De hoge plafonds, de witte muren en de tegelvloer in lichte natuursteen dragen bij tot de rust die de plek uitstraalt. Het ruime salon geeft enerzijds uit op de patio, anderzijds op het zwembad, via grote glaspartijen in klamplaag. De zwevende wand van de schoorsteen doet tevens dienst als projectiescherm. Het interieurontwerp, van de hand van Joëlle Lust, is chic en geraffineerd, uitgezuiverd, zonder strak te worden.

morellet

The kitchen, which opens onto the dining room, combines functionality and aesthetics, in harmony with the carefully selected furniture.

L'espace cuisine, ouvert sur la salle à manger, allie fonctionnalité et esthétisme, l'intégrant au mobilier environnant.

De keukenruimte, die uitgeeft op de eetkamer, verzoent functionaliteit met esthetische imperatieven, in harmonie met het omringende meubilair.

The office opens onto the patio and has a fine view of the dining room, the sitting room and the swimming pool.

Le bureau s'ouvre sur le patio et dispose, par transparence, d'une vue sur la salle à manger, le salon et la piscine.

Het bureau geeft uit op de patio en zorgt, door de transparantie, voor een uitstekend zicht op de eetkamer, het salon en het zwembad.

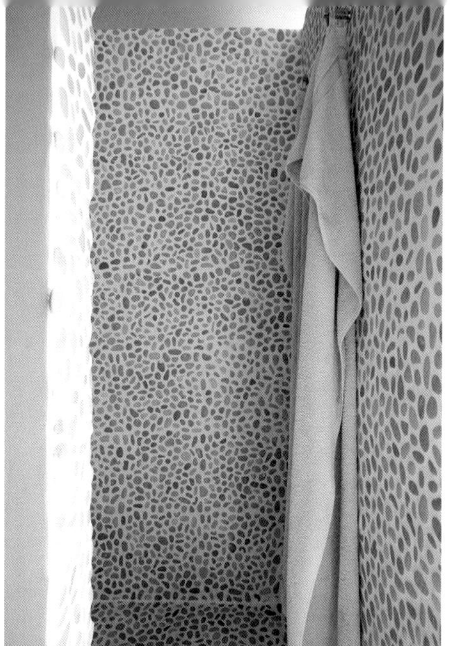

The central block, which contains the dressing room, provides a separation between the bedroom and the bathroom. A large shower room, with pebbles and bathtub, with a view of the surrounding woodland.

L'îlot central, renfermant le dressing, sépare la chambre de la salle de bains. Grand espace douche en galets et baignoire avec vue sur la forêt environnante.

Het centrale eiland, dat de dressing herbergt, zorgt voor de scheiding tussen de slaapkamer en de badkamer. Grote doucheruimte, met keien en badkuip, met zicht op het bos in de omtrek.

ADDRESSES

ADRESSES

ADRESSEN

Collection Privée
Gilles Pellerin / Nicolette Schouten

Architecture :
9, rue des Etats-Unis
F – 06400 Cannes
T +33 (0)4 97 06 94 94
F +33 (0)4 97 06 94 97
gilles@collection-privee.com

Decoration :
3, rue des Etats-Unis
F – 06400 Cannes
T +33 (0)4 93 99 23 22
F +33 (0)4 93 39 99 89
nicolette@collection-privee.com

Valbonne :
15, Faubourg du St-Esprit
F – 06560 Valbonne
T +33 (0)4 93 40 20 00
F +33 (0)4 93 40 20 04
valbonne@collection-privee.com

www.collection-privee.com

Designer's Studio
Josselin Fleury
21, rue Boulegon
F – 13100 Aix-en-Provence
T +33 (0)4 42 23 30 34
F +33 (0)4 42 96 07 41
www.designers-studio.com
contact@designers-studio.com

De Vos Projects
Christel De Vos
christel@devos-projects.be

Ebony Interiors

64, Bd. Malesherbes
F – 75008 Paris
T +33 (0)1 42 93 75 06
F +33 (0)1 42 93 70 24
paris@ebony-interiors.com

132, avenue Louise
B – 1050 Bruxelles
T +32 (0)2 646 86 02
F +32 (0)2 649 52 61
ebony@ebony-interiors.com

www.ebony-interiors.com

Kallos Turin Architects

37 Pottery Lane
London W11 4LY
UK
T +44 207 229 5840

3035 Pacific Avenue
San Francisco, CA 94115
USA

www.kallosturin.com
info@kallosturin.com

Marc Lust Architecture
T +33 (0)4 94 55 57 51
F +33 (0)4 94 55 57 52
marc.lust@wanadoo.fr

PUBLISHER
BETA-PLUS publishing
Termuninck 3
B - 7850 Enghien
www.betaplus.com

PHOTOGRAPHERS
Jo Pauwels,
except p. 124-139 Dennis Gilbert / View Pictures Ltd

DESIGN
Polydem - Nathalie Binart

TRANSLATION
Laura Watkinson (English)
Txt-Ibis (français)

ISBN 13 :
English version:
CONTEMPORARY LIVING IN PROVENCE & COTE D'AZUR
978-90-77213-96-4

Version française:
DEMEURES CONTEMPORAINES EN PROVENCE & COTE D'AZUR
978-2-930367-53-8

Nederlandstalige versie:
HEDENDAAGS WONEN IN PROVENCE & COTE D'AZUR
978-90-77213-95-7

Printed in China.